Uncle Switch

LOONY LIMERICKS

Other books by X. J. Kennedy

The Beasts of Bethlehem
illustrated by Michael McCurdy

Brats
illustrated by James Watts

Drat These Brats!
illustrated by James Watts

The Forgetful Wishing Well:
  Poems for Young People
illustrated by Monica Incisa

Fresh Brats
illustrated by James Watts

Ghastlies, Goops & Pincushions:
  Nonsense Verse
illustrated by Ron Barrett

The Kite That Braved Old Orchard Beach:
  Year-Round Poems for Young People
illustrated by Marian Young

Margaret K. McElderry Books

Uncle Switch

LOONY LIMERICKS

by
X. J. Kennedy

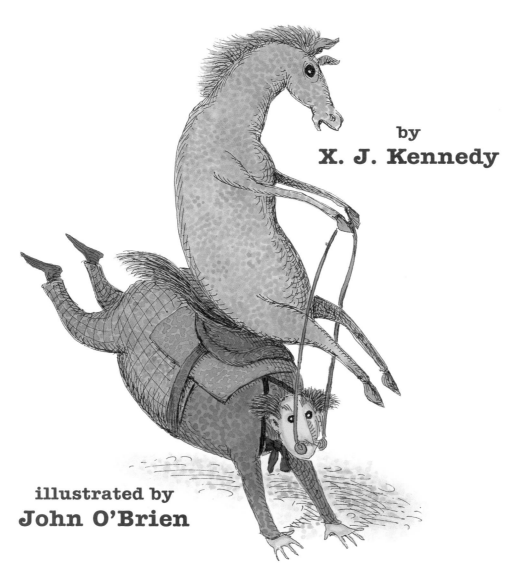

illustrated by
John O'Brien

MARGARET K. McELDERRY BOOKS

MARGARET K. MCELDERRY BOOKS
25 YEARS • 1972–1997

Text copyright © 1997 by X. J. Kennedy
Illustrations copyright © 1997 by John O'Brien

Margaret K. McElderry Books
An imprint of Simon & Schuster Children's Publishing Division
1230 Avenue of the Americas
New York, New York 10020

Book design by Ann Bobco

The text of this book is set in American Typewriter Bold.
The illustrations were rendered in ink and watercolors.

Printed in Hong Kong by South China Printing Co. (1988) Ltd.

10 9 8 7 6 5 4 3 2 1

Library of Congress Cataloging-in-Publication Data
Kennedy, X. J.
Uncle Switch : loony limericks by X. J. Kennedy ; illustrated by John O'Brien.
p.   cm.
Summary: A collection of limericks about Uncle Switch,
an eccentric who does everything topsy-turvy.
ISBN 0-689-80967-0
1. Eccentrics and eccentricities—Juvenile poetry. 2. Children's poetry, American.
3. Humorous poetry, American. 4. Limericks, Juvenile.
[1. Limericks. 2. Humorous poetry. 3. American poetry.]
I. O'Brien, John, 1953-   ill. II. Title.
PS3521.E563U53   1997
811'.54—dc20
96-888
CIP
AC

To Marilyn Marlow
—X. J. K.

To my father's granddaughter, Tess
—J. O.

Crack of dawn. Uncle Switch milks the pup,
Walks the Jersey cow, sloshes a cup
    Full of hot exercise,
    Reads two fresh eggs, and fries
All the morning news sunny side up.

Other mornings, this turned-around man
Downs a jug of milk, pours raisin bran,
   Toasts and butters his hair,
   Breaks an egg on his chair,
And goes scrambling about in the pan.

My, how well Uncle Switch fixed the clock's
Little problem! It now sits and rocks
    In his favorite chair
    While with hands in midair
Uncle points and cuckoos and tick-tocks.

Uncle Switch, as he swam in the brook,
Rashly swallowed a worm on a hook,
But the fillet of sole
Who was holding the pole
Declared, "Shucks, he's too dinky to cook."

Uncle Switch, wearing whiskers and fur,
Is determined to practice his purr
   And solicits advice
   On how best to catch mice
From a cat he addresses as "Sir."

And whenever a house mouse he sees,
Lets it scamper off free as the breeze
      While with deafening SNAP
      He sits down on a trap
And, imprisoned there, nibbles on cheese.

Uncle Switch has this tree whose routine
Is as mixed up as any I've seen:
    Apples ripe, red, and round
     Jump right up off the ground,
Fasten fast to a branch, and turn green.

Howland Hound can write stories and sketch,
Draw with crayons and paint, sculpt, and etch,
   And across Mucky Crick
   He keeps throwing a stick
Which he's teaching his master to fetch.

"Bath time, Howland! Begin, if you please!"—
Uncle's hound dog gets down on his knees
   And dunks Unk in the tub
   For a good sudsy scrub,
Then applies some white powder for fleas.

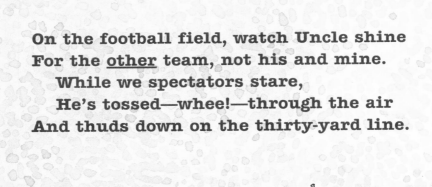

On the football field, watch Uncle shine
For the <u>other</u> team, not his and mine.
   While we spectators stare,
    He's tossed—whee!—through the air
And thuds down on the thirty-yard line.

When a thirsty mosquito in flight
Whistles down in the dead of the night
   To our uncle's sleep couch,
    The poor insect cries, "Ouch!"
And starts scratching an Uncle Switch bite.

Uncle Switch grumbles, "Every time I
Take a swat at that bluebottle fly,
    The smart little rotter
    Grabs ahold of the swatter
And he bops me KERSMACK in the eye."

Pedaling lickety-split down the pike
(In reverse, of course), Unk hears a shrike
    From the sky shriek, "At last
    You have got going fast,
But I fear you've forgotten your bike."

As a sitter, is anyone droller
Than our Unk? When he sits Bonnie Bowler,
    All the neighbors cry, "Yipe!
    Baby's puffing a pipe!
There she goes, pushing Switch in her stroller!"

Uncle Switch, at the beach for a swim,
Never jumps in. Instead, it's his whim
   On his blanket to lie
   Till the tide rises high—
He insists that the sea come to <u>him</u>.

What our Uncle Switch best likes to do
Is trade places with apes in the zoo.
On a swaying trapeze
He sits searching for fleas,
Peels bananas, and chitters at you.

Uncle says, "What an awful impasse!
All my cows claim their diet lacks class.
   Well, I won't be a meanie,
   I'll serve 'em linguini
And grab me a mouthful of grass."

When, by munching hard, Uncle gets through
Mowing meadowgrass—hear the man moo!—
    He exclaims with a snort,
    "Shucks, I've cut it too short!"—
So he sticks it all back on with glue.

When his frog Freddy sings, Uncle croaks,
And he blubbers when told funny jokes.
      Peeling onions, he laughs,
      And he snaps photographs
Of his camera to send to its folks.

Uncle Switch always follows a firm
Rule for feeding the birds: With a squirm
   He'll squeeze into their nest,
    Openmouthed as the rest,
Till the mom robin brings him a worm.